Windfall

IRISH NATURE POEMS
TO INSPIRE AND CONNECT

Jane Clarke is the author of three poetry collections, *The River* (2015), *When the Tree Falls* (2019) and *A Change in the Air* (2023) published by Bloodaxe Books. Jane received the Listowel Writers' Week Poem of the Year Award 2016, the Hennessy Literary Award for Poetry 2016 and the Ireland Chair of Poetry Travel Award 2022. Her poetry reflects the interdependence of people, place and nature while exploring loss and change, both personal and cultural. She grew up on a farm in Co. Roscommon and now lives with her wife in the uplands of Co. Wicklow.

Jane Carkill is an illustrator and textile designer living in the heart of The Burren in County Clare on the west coast of Ireland. She studied Fine Art Textiles at the School of Design and Creative Arts in Atlantic Technological University. She is fascinated by natural ephemeral beauty and intricate detail and combines a love of folklore, narration, myth and story with a precise style of illustration to capture an essence in nature that is both magical and nostalgic. Flora and fauna are the ultimate inspiration for her work, which portrays her everyday experience in the countryside.

Windfall

IRISH NATURE POEMS
TO INSPIRE AND CONNECT

Edited by   Illustrated by
JANE CLARKE   JANE CARKILL

HACHETTE
BOOKS
IRELAND

First published in Ireland in 2023 by
HACHETTE BOOKS IRELAND

1

Cataloguing in Publication Data is available from the British Library

ISBN: 978 1 399729611

Book design and typesetting: Slick Fish Design, Dublin
Printed and bound in Italy by L.E.G.O. Spa

Hachette Books Ireland's policy is to use papers that are natural, renewable and
recyclable products and made from wood grown in sustainable forests.
The logging and manufacturing processes are expected to conform to the
environmental regulations of the country of origin.

Hachette Books Ireland
8 Castlecourt Centre
Castleknock
Dublin 15, Ireland
A division of Hachette UK Ltd
Carmelite House, 50 Victoria Embankment, EC4Y 0DZ

www.hachettebooksireland.ie

MIX
Paper | Supporting
responsible forestry
FSC
www.fsc.org   FSC® C023419

To the caretakers, protectors and restorers
of our threatened habitats and species.

Contents

Woods and Trees

Birds

Lakes, Rivers & the Sea

Animals

Hills and Mountains

In the Garden

The Land

Foreword

I walk down through a hazel wood to swim. In the lacy light under the trees, I find bluebells in the spring, huge ferns in the summer, nuts in the autumn. It's magical, and because of the famous Yeats' line which actually begins this anthology, it feels mythical. That identification with nature which is part of Irish culture can be found in the song of our first poet, Amergin, who is said to have declared as he set foot on the shore near Waterville:

Am gaeth i m-muir,
Am tond trethan,
*Am fuaim mara**

Am wind on sea,
Am wave-swelling,
Am ocean's voice**

A few miles from where I live in County Carlow are the woods of St Mullins. Legend says it was here that Mad Sweeney, the king of Dal-Arie in Ulster – who was turned into a half-man half-bird by St Ronan – eventually found sanctuary. Our landscape holds our stories, our beliefs. Indeed, we have long identified God with nature. It's there in 'The Deer's Cry', the St Patrick's Breastplate hymn, which has inspired so many composers including Arvo Pärt and Shaun Davey:

> I arise today, through
> The strength of heaven,
> The light of the sun,
> The radiance of the moon.

I would even argue that it's there in the one hymn that most Irish people over fifty can sing, 'Queen of the May', which begins: 'Bring flowers of the fairest'. It's a hymn to Mary but, for all its Victorian sentiment, isn't it also a song to a Goddess of Spring and fertility?

This anthology captures the joy we take in nature but there's also grief at the damage we have done to it. When I walk the Barrow track now, I see the invasive Himalayan balsam taking over from purple loosestrife and meadowsweet. Trees dead from imported ash disease haunt the banks. The river itself, which teemed with salmon in my lifetime, is home now mainly to coarse fish. Most of our bird species are in trouble.

What is the role of the poet in face of such carelessness and destruction? To record what's still left? To write elegies for what's lost? Poets should do what poets always do: to say the unsayable, to restore in us a sense of the natural world which has been dulled or even lost through the urbanising of life and the destructiveness of modern farming methods. Poets can take something simple and local like a hazel wood and make its very name ring with wonder. That's what poets can do.

– Olivia O'Leary

*   From the medieval Irish version of the poem as printed in Unde Scribitur, the book brought out to mark the first Amergin Solstice Poetry Gathering in Waterville in 2018.
**   The English translation is by Paddy Bushe from the same publication.

Introduction

Windfall spans over a century of Irish nature poetry from the early 1900s to the present day. In gathering together these vivid, moving and memorable poems, I have sought to illuminate the ways in which they are inspired by the beauty and diversity of the natural world around us and also its resilience and fragility. Writing out of awe, love, grief and gratitude, the poets awaken us to the birds, animals, rivers, trees and wildflowers with which we share this island. The poems are arranged by species and habitat into seven sections, though there is inevitable overlap because everything in the natural world is interrelated.

In our time of environmental crisis, poetry has a unique role to play as spiritual witness to the loss that threatens everything we value. It nurtures imagination, evokes care and inspires action by connecting us to the natural world around us. It helps us sustain hope and find the courage we need to live differently. While paying homage to our diverse species and habitats these poems also, directly or indirectly, draw attention to the damage we are inflicting on them.

Freda Laughton's 'Now Linnet', written in the 1940s, holds a memory of abundant nature. Jessica Traynor's 'Swarm' mourns the rapid disappearance of bees while Seamus Heaney's celebration of the humble alder ends with a prescient exhortation: 'Plant it, plant it, / Streel head in the rain.' Jane Robinson reenvisages our relationship with waste land: '… life / blossoming in the stony places'. James Harpur's tribute to 'Roscommon Rain' is timely in its reminder that while we are part of nature, it has agency beyond our ken and control. In the way that poems accrue new meanings over time, Louis MacNeice's song of lost love, 'The Sunlight on the Garden', can now be read as a lament for our environment.

From its origins as an oral art form, Irish poetry has always and ever engaged with nature. Our first known poem, composed by the poet chieftain Amergin, celebrates the unity and interdependence of all things, a concept found at the heart of today's environmental movement as well as in indigenous spirituality through the ages. The relatively unknown Susan L. Mitchell, a contemporary of W.B. Yeats, gives us an arrestingly lyrical version of this ancient incantation: 'I buzz in the dizzy fly, I crawl in the creeping things. / I croak in the frog's throat, and fly on the bird's wings.'

How we turned to poetry and the natural world for solace during the coronavirus lockdowns was particularly striking but we have always done this in times of personal and communal crisis. Perhaps it is because both poetry and nature provide moments of respite and offer the companionship and perspective that help us create meaning and feel less alone. Seán Hewitt expresses this in the closing lines of 'Wild Garlic': the 'world is dark / but the wood is full of stars' while in her poem 'Peace' almost a hundred years' earlier, Eva Gore-Booth praised the hills that still the soul. In 'A Merlin in the Sheefry's' Martin Dyar captures the mysterious depth of what a landscape can mean to us: 'There is a feeling that is equal to the land, / a sense of self that is the journey's length.'

The anthology demonstrates how nature helps us give expression to our emotions at some of the most important times of our lives; when a grandchild comes into this world in Michael Longley's 'The Leveret' or when a father leaves this world in Paul Durcan's 'Staring Out the Window Three Weeks after His Death'. Leanne O'Sullivan evokes the healing to be found in 'That first days of springtime thaw' and Paula Meehan welcomes spring after a winter in which 'hope had died'.

Many of the poets bring the keen observation of a naturalist to their subject. Though herons are a common sight throughout this island few of us will have studied them as closely as the Donegal poet Francis Harvey. He presents the idiosyncrasy of this iconic bird with stunning verbal agility. Gail McConnell details the intricate workings of a worm while expressing wonder at how this tiny being shapes our everyday world. With reverential attention Mark Roper evokes the miracle of an owl in flight.

There are poems here that subtly explore the social and political dilemmas of their time, such as Winifred Letts' 'Dead', Austin Clarke's 'The Lost Heifer,' Annemarie Ní Churreáin's 'Border', Michael McKimm's 'The Land League' and Eoghan Wall's 'Up the Border'. Other poems explore how seeing ourselves reflected in nature helps us recognise who we are and what we cherish at different times in our lives; the teenage boy in Tara Bergin's 'Stag-Boy', the older couple in Thomas McCarthy's 'Falcons Hunting': 'Such love / Between falcon and falcon is impossibly human'. Those we love are revealed to us anew in how they respond to nature, as in Kevin Graham's 'The Lesson' when a father observes his young son's tenderness towards an injured bird or in Katie Donovan's 'Cows' where a daughter '… has fallen in love with cows.'

The history of our connection with nature is embedded in our poetry as well as in our myths, legends and folklore. Yeats evokes both the God of youth and love and the Celtic association of hazel with inspiration and divination in 'The Song of Wandering Aengus'. Nidhi Zak/Aria Eipe responds to this much-loved poem with her ethereal 'wandersong'. Eleanor Hooker's poem for a loved one who is ill calls on the magic healing of nature as rooted in our folklore: 'For the quicken tree is a hoary charm, / and quickening, its sap and store'.

Whether living in a city, a town or up a boreen many Irish

people's most intimate encounters with nature are in their gardens. Eavan Boland expresses the wealth of imaginative possibilities there: 'Things are getting ready / to happen / out of sight' as does Geraldine Mitchell in 'Sea Garden': 'This garden's space / enough to stage small / miracles…'

The poems in the final section explore our complex relationship with the land that sustains us. Eiléan Ní Chuilleanáin's 'Woman Shoeing a Horse' depicts with painterly detail a way of life at a particular time in a particular place, 'the horse in the open air clanking his feet.' This time is gone but the poem allows the reader to linger at '…the path to the stile.' Patrick Kavanagh praises the sacramental and creative potential of the 'Eternity of April clay'. Bernard O'Donoghue recalls the wonder of a childhood day on the farm while Michael Hartnett rails against the hardship his grandmother endured on a few poor acres. Nessa O'Mahony reminds us of what is on offer in unexpected places: 'But if you hold your ground, / if the wind is in the right direction, / the gate will sing to you'. Frances Ledwidge longs for the 'little fields of home' when he is trapped in the merciless destruction of the First World War whereas Paul Muldoon's haunting poem, 'Why Brownlee Left', questions why Brownlee abandoned all that should have made him content.

Jane Carkill's captivating illustrations respond to the poems with empathy and imagination. The intricate detail of her work reveals a keen observation of animals, plants and habitats. What the poets do with words, she does with drawings and watercolours, attending to, celebrating and cherishing Irish nature in its marvellous diversity.

It has been my privilege to select poems from the rich heritage of Irish nature poetry over the past century. I was struck by how many Irish poets, outside of those known as 'nature poets', are inspired by the natural world. It revealed to me that our relationship with nature is embedded in what Seamus Heaney called the 'secret crevices of individual consciousness'. My only regret is the many wonderful poems I did not have space to include. I hope that readers will find pleasure, excitement, companionship and solace here, whether discovering poems for the first time or rediscovering old favourites. Above all, I hope they will encounter the riches of Irish nature anew in this windfall and experience the sense of inspiration and connection celebrated by Moya Cannon in 'Bilberry Blossom on Seefin':

all the ringing promise
of that blossom and leaf

– Jane Clarke

Woods and Trees

Plant it, plant it,
Streel-head in the rain.

from 'Planting the Alder', Seamus Heaney

The Song of Wandering Aengus

I went out to the hazel wood,
Because a fire was in my head,
And cut and peeled a hazel wand,
And hooked a berry to a thread;
And when white moths were on the wing,
And moth-like stars were flickering out,
I dropped the berry in a stream
And caught a little silver trout.

When I had laid it on the floor
I went to blow the fire a-flame,
But something rustled on the floor,
And someone called me by my name:
It had become a glimmering girl
With apple blossom in her hair
Who called me by my name and ran
And faded through the brightening air.

Though I am old with wandering
Through hollow lands and hilly lands,
I will find out where she has gone,
And kiss her lips and take her hands;
And walk among long dappled grass,
And pluck till time and times are done,
The silver apples of the moon,
The golden apples of the sun.

William Butler Yeats

wandersong

some day, love, go into the wood,
and cast your sights out far ahead,
look closely for a flash of wand,
squint: conjuring of silver thread;
elbow emerged of feathered wing,
ribs stitched together inside out,
a goddess rising from the stream
skinkissed by darting silver trout.

race now, across the valley floor
footsparks that set a heart aflame,
lie with her on the muddrunk floor,
and call this creature by her name:
sweet Caer that swanned into a girl
lakedrops still heavy in her hair
dripping over the fields she ran
carolling through the sunspun air.

some day, love, go out wandering
through this folk lore, these spirit lands,
where whispered tell of tales long gone,
and fading light colours your hands;
pause there among the foxtail grass,
here: fix your wings, they've come undone,
and lift your shoulders to the moon,
and turn your face – full – to the sun.

Nidhi Zak/Aria Eipe

The Quicken Tree

for Margaret Griffin

Berries bloom across the landscape
of your body, ripen to purpura.

The physician says petechiae, says blood
words that snag the thin winter air.

I have sown a rowan inside me,
nourished it in my woodland bones

for two hundred years, its berries
bud at my fingertips, red-blistered.

An chéad lá de Bhealtaine, do mhí bhreithe,
beidh an deatach ón gcéad tine as caorthann.

And I will crush my flowers as a cure for you,
from my flushed berries, stir a brew for you,

I will pestle and mortar my leaves for you,
add spice and light scented-sticks for you,

from my wood I will carve a settle for you,
from my bark I will dye my eyes for you –
For the quicken tree is a hoary charm,
and quickening, its sap and store.

Eleanor Hooker

Planting the Alder

For the bark, dulled argent, roundly wrapped
And pigeon-collared.

For the splitter-splatter, guttering
Rain-flirt leaves.

For the snub and clot of the first green cones,
Smelted emerald, chlorophyll.

For the scut and scat of cones in winter,
So rattle-skinned, so fossil-brittle.

For the alder-wood, flame-red when torn
Branch from branch.

But mostly for the swinging locks
Of yellow catkins.

Plant it, plant it,
Streel-head in the rain.

Seamus Heaney

Trees Abiding

Battered as they've been by fire rain incessant wind
    this ash and sycamore still put out green shoots and
        leaves
that whisper in any passing breeze and make perch
    and resting post for blackbird goldcrest magpie wren
that flash as shadows among them and wait
    for Brother Bread to scatter morning manna on gravel
when they'll clutch at these trunks that are all scarred by
    circumstance
    but which they know only as the state and nature
of the world they pass through as it passes through them
    with nothing more (or less) than the usual swerve
from catastrophe to appetite and back – and so they flutter
    down to our earth and feed when they need and risk each
        moment
for the moment: quick in the lichen-lit twisted limbs
    half-ravaged but still upright still abiding
of these trees.

Eamon Grennan

A Plum Tree

for Fiona

When the tree falls, how can the shadow stand?
 – Mary Lavin, 'In the Middle of the Fields'

We planted two we meant to mean ourselves,
turned so that the longest branch of each
appeared to be reaching towards the other
at the end of the garden, across grass and air.

In their second season, when one's limbs bowed
with young fruit and wasps swarmed to feast,
specks appeared on the tips of the other's leaves
and the white flesh beneath the bark turned brown.

We forgot if the lost one had been me or you
and spoke of replacing it but didn't.
Grass filled in the bare patch. Desiccated roots

and the thin trunk went up like tinder.
A loppers even off the reaching branch.
The one that prospered came to mean the two.

Tom French

Calling To Me Through the Woods

I have gone out searching for you
in amongst the thick-knit spruces
at the place where the fire-break peters
in the hours when birds sleep
and long-boned Alsatians crouch
alongside last night's bonfire.

I have carried no torch
for fear of waking the living
just bluebells
and foxgloves and rosemary
and the torn part of me that aches
for your stout-hearted stillness.

But you are in hiding
fastened with the moss, maybe,
to the river wall,
upstanding with the heron
or endurance swimming
with the wisest salmon
back bravely to the dark Atlantic salt.

Shirley McClure

Tree III

When I was small trees grew wild
In saltwater. They came in on the tide
For roof beams, a chair for a child.

I had a fiddle carved from windfall.
When the bow scraped out a few tunes
A sweeter note echoed under the keel.

Mary O'Malley

Wild Garlic

Out in the copse after rain
(too late after dark to be here).
Warm soil, woodlice dripping
from the underside of leaves.

I root down to the tender stalks
and twist them free – soaked petals
dip and touch my arm, kernels
of bud, itch of foliage, of wildness

on my skin. The plants are carrying
the smell, earth-rich, too heavy
to lift above head-height, and my boots
and jeans are bleached with it.

I turn home, and all across the floor
the spiked white flowers
light the way. The world is dark
but the wood is full of stars.

Seán Hewitt

Birds

Now linnet, finch and willow-wren,
Their quilted nests must fill again,

from 'Now Linnet', Freda Laughton

Now Linnet

Now linnet, finch and willow-wren,
Their quilted nests must fill again,
And buds must tie their new green bows
On thin twigs where the sharp thorn grows,
And in its cradle sleeps the rose.

Now young winds spiral down the shell
Of distance where the hills of Mourne
Beyond the reaches of the Lough
Have pursed their lips into a horn.

Now cuckoo's egg in strange nest lies.
Small leaves sprout wings, and little flies
Float by on rainbow petals. Skies
Grow tender as they hear the lark
Strip one by one the scales of dark.

Freda Laughton

Owl

is that part of a tree
which peels away at dusk
to float out over a field.

Comes under cloak of bark.
Not to be told from a branch.
Finds this to her liking.

Her hunt the stillest of listen.
Open air shaking out
a sudden cloth, her kill.

By day a feathered flask,
where mouse and vole
are silently rendered.

No good the sun knocking
at her door. Only dark knows
how to open her wings.

Mark Roper

Dead

In misty cerements they wrapped the word
My heart had feared so long: dead... dead... I heard
But marvelled they could think the thing was true
Because death cannot be for such as you.
So while they spoke kind words to suit my need
Of foolish idle things my heart took heed,
Your racquet and worn-out tennis shoe,
Your pipe upon the mantel,–then a bird
Upon the wind-tossed larch began to sing
And I remembered how one day in Spring
You found the wren's nest in the wall and said
"Hush!... listen! I can hear them quarrelling..."
The tennis court is marked, the wrens are fled,
But you are dead, beloved, you are dead.

Winifred M. Letts

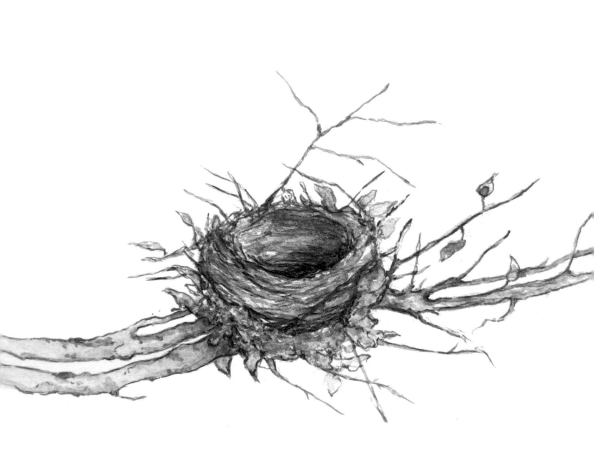

Heron

In memory of Beatrice Behan

was assembled out of bits and scraps, not made.
Like one of those early flying machines held together
    with glue and twine.
His undercarriage is an afterthought sticking out behind.
He is all wings and no fuselage and probably hollow inside.
Finn could have blown him off the palm of his hand.

He creaks into flight. The wind buffets him, gives him
a bumpy ride: it seems he must somehow end up
in a twisted heap of canvas and struts on the mountainside.
But no: he tacks into weathers with a prow that rises
    and falls in the swell.
The ghost of the pterodactyl haunts him in every cell.

He alights: furls his wings like a wet umbrella, settles
    rapt and murderous,
drying out in the wind and sun on the edge of a tarn
or hunched over a pool in the burn pretending he's
a blind one-legged beggar-man or a mystic
    communing with God.
Too late, too late for the fish or frog when it realises
    he's not an old cod.

Heron invented slow motion long before the movies came but
allows himself the lightening of his pickaxe
        for the killing game.
Heron's the icon of the silences beyond the last tongues
of land where the islands float and quiver like mirages
        in the light,
he's the hermit who daily petrifies himself in the reeds
        of the penitential lake,
the logo of the lonely places past the last sheep and
        the last house,
the El Greco or Modigliani doodle in a remote corner
        of the evening sky where
the newsprint of distant waders swims before the eye,
heron's that sudden outlandish screech you hear at midnight
in the water meadows as he changes into the wrong gear.

Francis Harvey

The Lesson

On finding a sparrow with a twisted wing
struggling on the patio he scooped it up like gold,
put his hands together as if he were praying
and carried it to the tinder shanty of the shed.

There among the implements and shelves of scrap
he found an old lunchbox and eased the bird down
on a bed made out of newspaper. Awe had sapped
him of nearly all his strength but the worried frown

knitted on his brow didn't drop a stitch. The moon
came out and still he stared at the injured bird,
the young mother in him bristling. No one
knew where he'd got to and when he finally heard

his called out name he pushed the black door
bright. Feathers glanced the tip of his shoulder.

Kevin Graham

Fáinleoga

Bhuail na bioráin binneas ceoil ón gciúnas,
greimeanna ag tuirlingt amhail fáinleoga
i scuaine ár sreang ag fáinne an lae,
iad ag faire ar shnáithín olla á shníomh
ina ghúinín cróchbhuí, gan lúb ar lár,

déanta di siúd
a d'fhan, is
a d'imigh léi
i bhfaiteadh na súl.

Sínte spréite i m'aonar
i bhfuacht an ospidéil,
cuimlím míne, gile
an ghúna le leathleiceann liom.
Scaoilim leis an tsnaidhm
ligim le
                              lúb
                ar
        lúb

snáithe silte
fáinleoga ag titim as radharc
le luí na gréine.

Fásann an liathróid olla
i mo lámh: lúbha, liatha, lán.

Doireann Ní Ghríofa

Swallows

The knitting needles drew song from silence,
little stitches following each another
as dawn swallows gather on a wire,
peering at a skirt of yellow wool
that grew bright as a bruise, becoming

a dress
for a girl who came
and left
too soon.

Stretched in a narrow bed,
I lie in a corridor, alone. Cold,
I hold the small dress to my cheek
a moment, then unbind the knot,
and release

                            stitch
                  after
         stitch

each unpicked, as swallows vanish
at dusk to some unfathomable land,
far from us.

I hold this soft unravelment as it grows,
and O, it grows, this un-wound wool. It grows. Dull. Full.

Doireann Ní Ghríofa

Blackbird in Dun Laoghaire

There's a blackbird in Dun Laoghaire
When I'm walking with my sons
Through the laneways
Called 'The Metals'
By the train-tracks.

And he sings among the dandelions
And bottle-tops and stones,
Serenading purple ivy,
Weary tree-trunks.

And I have it in my head
That I can recognise his song,
Pick him out,
I mean distinct
From all his flock-mates.

Impossible, I know.
Heard one blackbird, heard them all.
But there are times
He whistles up a recollection.

There's a blackbird in Dun Laoghaire –
And I'm suddenly a kid,
Asking where from here to Sandycove
My youngest sister hid.

I'm fourteen this Easter.
My job to mind her.
Good Friday on the pier –
And I suddenly can't find her.

The sky like a bruise
By the lighthouse wall.
We were playing hide-and-seek.
Is she lost? Did she fall?
There's a blackbird in Dun Laoghaire
And the terror's like a wave
Breaking hard on a hull,
And the peoples' faces grave

As Yeats on a banknote.
Stern as the mansions
Of Killiney in the distance,
As the pier's granite stanchions,
And Howth is a drowned child
Slumped in Dublin Bay,
And my heart is a drum
And the breakers gull-grey.

The baths. It starts raining.
The People's Park.
And my tears and the terns,
And the dogs' bitter bark.
There's a blackbird in Dun Laoghaire,
And I pray to him, then,
For God isn't here,
In a sobbed Amen.

And she waves from the bandstand,
Her hair in damp strings,
And the blackbird arises
With a clatter of wings
From the shrubs by the teahouse,
Where old ladies dream
Of sailors and Kingstown
And Teddy's ice-cream.

And we don't say a word
But cling in the mizzle,
And the whistle of the bird
Getting lost in the drizzle.
Mercy weaves her nest
In the wildflowers and the leaves,
There are stranger things in heaven
Than a blackbird believes.

Joseph O'Connor

Kestrel

Took my eye into the air of himself
and threaded it,

sewing me to the sky
with his looped cycle of flight

up the gully,
then traced a noose

around a lowland belfry
and now, in the suburbs,

can needle a spot
above the apex of a gable,

draw the skein
in circles widening out,

and glide back
to the eye of his obsession.

Seán Lysaght

Night Sky in Tyrone

Maybe birds provide the eyes the dead look out of.
Or is it knots in furniture they queue up at

to spy from, bickering, whispering with shock
how grey her hair is now, how skinny he has got.

My sister thinks that portly robin on the lawn
is Dad come back to say hello, and he takes a little hop

out of sunlight into shade before alighting on
the compost bag and lengthily explaining everything

that we can see is his, his apple tree, his grass,
that patch of rhubarb he'd been about to cut back.

Why not. We finish up a bottle then another
and the evening's coming on, and then the night is here,

and we sit out underneath so much made known
that's always there – the depths of emptiness and fire.

Nick Laird

Falcons Hunting

Imperceptible disturbance there in the gloaming:

We raise our eyes to their ghostly presences,
A pair of falcons soaring above our windows –

See how steady they are in the air together,
Earth's most heavenly creatures taking the blue air

Of early June, as we are in the private hours
After Whitsun love-making. The crumpled

Sheets of feathery cloud, high as falcons,
Even higher, are love's unmistakeable signature;

And these great high creatures, double nibs of life
Creating a single brushstroke, Chinese calligraphers

Of a long romance, just bank together
And sail into a fresh up-draft. The conjugal air

They recognise, I'm sure, the sudden, uncalled for uplift
That gives an even higher viewpoint. Such love

Between falcon and falcon is impossibly human.

Thomas McCarthy

Lakes, Rivers and the Sea

I am still in my heart in search of safe harbour –
the wide shallow basin I've heard called a haven.

from 'Longboat at Portaferry', Siobhán Campbell

The Leveret

for my grandson, Benjamin

This is your first night in Carrigskeewaun.
The Owennadornaun is so full of rain
You arrived in Paddy Morrison's tractor,
A bumpy approach in your father's arms
To the cottage where, all of one year ago,
You were conceived, a fire-seed in the hearth.
Did you hear the wind in the fluffy chimney?
Do you hear the wind tonight, and the rain
And a shore bird calling from the mussel reefs?
Tomorrow I'll introduce you to the sea,
Little hoplite. Have you been missing it?
I'll park your chariot by the otters' rock
And carry you over seaweed to the sea.
There's a tufted duck on David's lake
With her sootfall of hatchlings, pompoms
A day old and already learning to dive.
We may meet the stoat near the erratic
Boulder, a shrew in his mouth, or the merlin
Meadow-pipit-hunting. But don't be afraid.
The leveret breakfasts under the fuchsia
Every morning, and we shall be watching.
I have picked wild flowers for you, scabious
And centaury in a jam-jar of water
That will bend and magnify the daylight.
This is your first night in Carrigskeewaun.

Michael Longley

Amergin

I buzz in the dizzy fly, I crawl in the creeping
    things.
I croak in the frog's throat and fly on the bird's
    wings.

I play on the keys of the brain, a thought goes
    here, goes there;
Bird or beast, it has bounds, but I am every-
    where.

I dip in the pools of the rocks and the minnow
    plays with me.
Finned I am like a fish, and merry children
    are we.

At the dumb call of the darkness I go to the
    ocean's side,
I stand on the docile beach and bridle the eager
    tide.

The fretted waters I hold in the hollow of my
    hand.
From my heart go fire and dew and the green
    and the brown land.

Susan L. Mitchell

The Five Senses

The steady hiss of the tilly,
The groaning rain barrel;

Boiled bollan,
Baled hay;

The fossil on the stone
Where the soap sits;

Tall moon-white daisies
On the bank, shaking,

And sea salt
In the sea mist.

Dermot Healy

The Trout

for Barrie Cooke

Flat on the bank I parted
Rushes to ease my hands
In the water without a ripple
And tilt them slowly downstream
To where he lay, tendril-light,
In his fluid sensual dream.

Bodiless lord of creation,
I hung briefly above him
Savouring my own absence,
Senses expanding in the slow
Motion, the photographic calm
That grows before action.

As the curve of my hands
Swung under his body
He surged with visible pleasure.
I was so preternaturally close
I could count every stipple
But still cast no shadow, until

The two palms crossed in a cage
Under the lightly pulsing gills.
Then (entering my own enlarged
Shape, which rode on the water)
I gripped. To this day I can
Taste his terror on my hands.

John Montague

Leaba Shíoda

Do chóireoinn leaba duit
i Leaba Shíoda
sa bhféar ard
faoi iomrascáil na gcrann
is bheadh do chraiceann ann
mar shíoda ar shíoda
sa doircheacht
am lonnaithe na leamhan.

Craiceann a shníonn
go gléineach thar do ghéaga
mar bhainne á dháil as crúiscíní
am lóin
is tréad gabhar ag gabháil thar chnocáin
do chuid gruaige
cnocáin ar a bhfuil faillte arda
is dhá ghleann atá domhain.

Is bheadh do bheola taise
ar mhilseacht shiúcra
tráthnóna is sinn ag spaisteoireacht
cois abhann
is na gaotha meala
ag séideadh thar an Sionna
is na fiúisí ag beannú duit
ceann ar cheann.

Na fiúisí ag ísliú
a gceanna maorga
ag umhlú síos don áilleacht
os a gcomhair
is do phriocfainn péire acu
mar shiogairlíní
is do mhaiseoinn do chluasa
mar bhrídeog.

Ó, chóireoinn leaba duit
i Leaba Shíoda
le hamhascarnach an lae
i ndeireadh thall
is ba mhór an pléisiúr dúinn
bheith géaga ar ghéaga
ag iomrascáil
am lonnaithe na leamhan.

Nuala Ní Dhomhnaill

Labysheedy (The Silken Bed)

I'd make a bed for you
in Labysheedy
in the tall grass
under the wrestling trees
where your skin
would be silk upon silk
in the darkness
when the moths are coming down.

Skin which glistens
shining over your limbs
like milk being poured
from jugs at dinnertime;
your hair is a herd of goats
moving over rolling hills,
hills that have high cliffs
and two ravines.

And your damp lips
would be as sweet as sugar
at evening and we walking
by the riverside
with honeyed breezes
blowing over the Shannon
and the fuchsias bowing down to you
one by one.

The fuchsias bending low
their solemn heads
in obeisance to the beauty
in front of them
I would pick a pair of flowers
as pendant earrings
to adorn you
like a bride in shining clothes.

O I'd make a bed for you
in Labysheedy,
in the twilight hour
with evening falling slow
and what a pleasure it would be
to have our limbs entwine
wrestling
while the moths are coming down.

Nuala Ní Dhomhnaill

Month's Mind

We don't know which ones we're meant to bring
so we settle on the yellows for all the sorrys
there are. We pick the smallest bunch. Full
of buds, but no flowers, we lay them to rest
in the river. Our slow footsteps mourn the dying
shadows as we walk back to the house together

and alone. Once home, we bury our good shoes
at the bottom of the wardrobe. We pour the tea
and unwrap plates of sandwiches and cake.
In low voices we talk a little about the life
you never lived, and the house you never lived in
is overwhelmed by all the people who didn't know to come.

Aoife Lyall

Longboat at Portaferry

At the mouth of the Lough, I approach by the narrows
from fast-running tides to the place of strong currents.

I have bided my time, observing the flux,
the seals and the plover beside me beguiled.

I am still in my heart in search of safe harbour –
the wide shallow basin I've heard called a haven.

Like the waders and geese, I come back each season,
a to-ing and fro-ing since nature began.

I can see us some springtime, both new-come and native,
bathed in the light of a ferry at sunrise

when the eelgrass and thrift, the aster and thyme
are budding and thriving in warmth re-arriving,

and along all the narrows are sponges and corals –
a riot of colour remembering to bloom.

Siobhán Campbell

Seals at High Island

The calamity of seals begins with jaws.
Born in caverns that reverberate
With endless malice of the sea's tongue
Clacking on shingle, they learn to bark back
In fear and sadness and celebration.
The ocean's mouth opens forty feet wide
And closes on a morsel of their rock.

Swayed by the thrust and backfall of the tide,
A dappled grey bull and a brindled cow
Copulate in the green water of a cove.
I watch from a cliff-top, trying not to move.
Sometimes they sink and merge into black shoals;
Then rise for air, his muzzle on her neck,
Their winged feet intertwined as a fishtail.

She opens her fierce mouth like a scarlet flower
Full of white seeds; she holds it open long
At the sunburst in the music of their loving;
And cries a little. But I must remember
How far their feelings are from mine marooned.
If there are tears at this holy ceremony
Theirs are caused by brine and mine by breeze.

When the great bull withdraws his rod, it glows
Like a carnelian candle set in jade.
The cow ripples ashore to feed her calf;
While an old rival, eyeing the deed with hate,
Swims to attack the tired triumphant god.
They rear their heads above the boiling surf,
Their terrible jaws open, jetting blood.

At nightfall they haul out, and mourn the drowned,
Playing to the sea sadly their last quartet,
An improvised requiem that ravishes
Reason, while ripping scale up like a net:
Brings pity trembling down the rocky spine
Of headlands, till the bitter ocean's tongue
Swells in their cove, and smothers their sweet song.

Richard Murphy

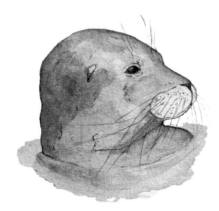

Achill

I lie and imagine a first light gleam in the bay
   After one more night of erosion and nearer the grave,
Then stand and gaze from a window at break of day
   As a shearwater skims the ridge of an incoming wave;
And I think of my son a dolphin in the Aegean,
   A sprite among sails knife-bright in a seasonal wind,
And wish he were here where currachs walk on the ocean
   To ease with his talk the solitude locked in my mind.

I sit on a stone after noon and consider the glow
   Of the sun through mist, a pearl bulb containédly fierce;
A rain-shower darkens the schist for a minute or so,
   Then it drifts away and the sloe-black patches disperse.
Croagh Patrick towers like Naxos over the water
   And I think of my daughter at work on her difficult art
And wish she were with me now between thrush and plover,
   Wild thyme and sea-thrift, to lift the weight from my heart.

The young sit smoking and laughing on the bridge at
      evening
   Like birds on a telephone pole or notes on a score.
A tin whistle squeals in the parlour, once more it is raining,
   Turfsmoke inclines and a wind whines under the door;
And I lie and imagine the lights going on in the harbour
   Of white-housed Náousa, your clear definition at night,
And wish you were here to upstage my disconsolate labour
   As I glance through a few thin pages and switch off the
      light.

Derek Mahon

Pier

Speak to our muscles of a need for joy.

W H Auden, 'Sonnets from China' (XVII)

Left at the lodge and park, snout to America.
Strip to togs, a shouldered towel, flip-flop over
the tarmac past the gangplanked rooted barge,
two upended rowboats and trawlers biding time.
Nod to a fisherman propped on a bollard,
exchange the weather, climb the final steps
up to the ridge. And then let fly. Push wide,
tuck up your knees so the blue nets hold you,
wide-open, that extra beat. Gulp cloud;
fling a jet-trail round your neck like a feather boa,
toss every bone and sinew to the plunge.
Enter the tide as if it were nothing,
really nothing, to do with you. Kick back.
Release your ankles from its coiled ropes;
slit water, drag it open, catch your breath.
Haul yourself up into August. Do it over,
raucously. Head first. This time, shout.

Vona Groarke

Riptide

I lost it to strong currents;
it slid over my cold knuckle
and got swept away before it sank,
though I stood chest high among tall waves
while you dived and dived to save it.
Every glint the sun hit
seemed to strike its shape,
as ebb jets carved the sand from underfoot,
till we had to cede it to the tide, and leave,
quite naked for its lack. No new gold ring
could bond *that* me, *that* you,
those strangers lost to time.

Amanda Bell

The Waste Land Recovers

The waste land recovers

when barnacles clutch tight again
to the tide-washed rocks, and seaweed
branches out of the stony rubbish;

when the heap of broken coral settles
and is sewn under by life billowing
in its image; when reef fish swim

where the sun beats, and an octopus
nestles in, safe under this red rock;
when your shadow at noon striding

behind you is a woman who sings
loud in the language of sea mammals;
when you carry a handful of water

in your cupped palms and, spilling
out of your arms, rumpled paper boats
made from government documents;

when the violet hour safely passes
and we draft a blueprint for joy, life
blossoming in the stony places.

Jane Robinson

Animals

Hares on the beat, hedgehogs on the ball,
deer drinking long in the late night lake-bar.

from 'Summer Yearn', Eithne Hand

Mare at Large

The mare
has lifted up into the sky, has cleared the hedge
and breached the next farm along.
All afternoon she will gallop freely
with her tail over her back;
she isn't minded to be caught.

She has jumped and she will gallop –
the mare who, finding your finger in her jaws,
will press the bone
and look at you
and stop.

A mare
is not a river,
is not a child jumping hedges
from the window of a train –
gather and reach, gather and reach,
jump the house, the factories and everything:
what is visible is jumpable, so long
as the striding's right.

A mare
is not a river. She will tire,
will take into her foam-slashed mouth
a carrot like a finger,
she will be caught.

But still, the mare has jumped the hedge
and breached the next farm along.
She has galloped all afternoon,
flags
flaunting in the wind.
This cannot be taken from her.

Miriam Gamble

The Watchers

We crouched and waited as the day ebbed off
and the close birdsong dwindled point by point,
nor daring the indulgence of a cough
or the jerked protest of a weary joint;
and when our sixty minutes had run by
and lost themselves in the declining light
we heard the warning snuffle and the sly
scuffle of mould, and, instantly, the white
long head thrust through the sighing undergrowth,
and the grey badger scrambled into view,
eager to frolic carelessly, yet loth
to trust the air his greedy nostrils drew;
awhile debated with each distant sound,
then, settling into confidence, began

to scratch his tough-haired side, to sniff the ground
without the threat of that old monster, man.
And as we watched him, gripped in our surprise,
that moment suddenly began to mean
more than a badger, and a row of eyes,
a stony brook, a leafy ditch between.
It was as if another nature came
close to my knowledge, but could not be known;
yet if I tried to call it by its name
would start, alarmed, and instantly be gone.

John Hewitt

The Drey

When the squirrel stands
        on her hind paws,
I see a pink line
        of swollen nipples.

Nearby
        there must be a drey
of babies waiting
        to sup her milk.

As I watch her
        I realise everything
I love
        is grey –

birches whispering
        to me all night
as they break the wall
        with hungry roots;

my mother,
        silvery in evening light
as she tugs
        weed from the pond;

the newt, a band
        of muscle and movement
she stoops to return
         to colourless water;

even Milena is grey
        at the temples,
eyes shadowed
        as she lies by me in bed

with the pewter cat
        who nudges a space
between our torsos,
        and rasps a purr.

When rain starts,
        I smell lavender and soil
and for a moment
        I am the squirrel

on the trellis, unpeeling
        dove-grey sunflower seeds
to turn
        into sweet milk.

Rosamund Taylor

Staring Out the Window Three Weeks after His Death

On the last day of his life as he lay comatose in the
    hospital bed
I saw that his soul was a hare which was poised
In the long grass of his body, ears pricked.
It sprang toward me and halted and I wondered if it
Could hear me breathing
Or if it could smell my own fear, which was,
Could he but have known it, greater than his
For plainly he was a just and playful man
And just and playful men are as brave as they are rare.
Then his cancer-eroded body appeared to shudder
As if a gust of wind blew through the long grass
And the hare of his soul made a U-turn
And began bounding away from me
Until it disappeared from sight into a dark wood
And I thought – that is the end of that,
I will not be seeing him again.
He died in front of me; no one else was in the room.
My eyes teemed with tears; I could not damp them down.
I stood up to walk around his bed
Only to catch sight again of the hare of his soul
Springing out of the wood into a beachy cove of sunlight

And I thought: Yes, that's how it is going to be from now on.
The hare of his soul always there, when I least expect it;
Popping up out of nowhere, sitting still.

Paul Durcan

Cows

She has fallen in love with cows:
their huge, mild bodies
that chew and stare,
the way they stand
with lowered, curious heads
beside their fuzzy young,
or lie, lazing on their haunches
in the sun.

She makes her way on tiny legs,
close as she dares,
she points her little fist,
lowing luxuriantly with pursed lips:
'Moo.' Then waits
for them to say it too.

She can spot them fields away,
forms of rust or black and white,
just seeing them
is immense joy guaranteed,
visual satiation, the answering
of a patent need.

The creatures barely heed
their worshipper: small bald witness
of their horned beauty.
They sway, munching and blowing,
twitching and lifting their tails
to emit
fascinating streams of stink.

When the summer heat
cools to evening,
they lose their torpor,
and out of the curvaceous caverns
of their grass-filled bellies
come bellows and roars
leaving her aghast and thrilled.

They bawl for the farmer
and his cheeky dog
to take them in,
relieve the swollen lactic sacs
of their creamy load.

After milking, she ignores
the sunset's pinkening shawl,
to rush for one last look,
her hands pulling up
on the low stone wall;
the languid hulks –
like statues in the trodden grass –
remain insensible
to her urgent bed-time call,
to her radiant bliss
that they are there at all.

Katie Donovan

Octopus

Mariners call them devil fish,
noting the eerie symmetry
of those nervy serpentine arms.
They resemble nothing so much
as a man's cowled head and shoulders.
Mostly they are sessile, and shy
as monsters, waiting in rock-clefts
or coral for a swimming meal.

They have long since abandoned their
skulls to the depths, and go naked
in this soft element, made of
a brain-sac and elephant eye.
The tenderness of their huge heads
makes them tremble at the shameful
intimacy of the killing
these ropes of sticky muscle do.

Females festoon their cavern roofs
with garlands of ripening eggs
and stay to tickle them and die.
Their reproductive holocaust
leaves them pallid and empty. Shoals
of shad and krill, like sheet lightning,
and the ravenous angelfish
consume their flesh before they die.

Caitríona O'Reilly

The Bat

Church doors wide open,
the bat came flying in
that October evening,

dark wings splayed,
swooped over the congregation
in packed pews,

across the silent altar,
stirring the air above
the celebrant,

drew a ripple from children
gathered for Communion,
levitated for their eyes.

Flew high as the rafters,
creature of night skies,
tiny claws quivered past

solemn readings from Isaiah,
the Gospel of St Mark?
Chose this occasion

to run amok,
turn the heads of girls
in best dresses,

small boys in long pants,
break all the rules,
eerily, to dance?

Catherine Phil MacCarthy

Stag-Boy

He enters the carriage with a roar –
He clatters in wildly and fills up the carriages with heat,
running through the train, staining the floor
with hooves dirty from the street;
tearing at the ceilings with his new branched horns,
banging his rough sides against the seats and
the women, who try to look away; Gallant!
He sings hard from his throat,
his young belling tearing at his chest,
pushing at his boy-throat.

Stag-boy –

the train's noise hums in his ears,
sharp and high like crickets pulsing
in the tall grass,
and he wounds it with his horns,
maddened like a stung bull,
pushing up his head,
pushing up his mouth for his mother's teat:
Where is her beestings?
Where is the flowered mug she used to warm his milk in?

No good, no good now.

He's smashing out of the train door,
he's banging his hooves in the industrial air,
he's galloping through the city squares,
and drinking from a vandalised spring –

And still his mother walks through the house,
crying: *Stag-boy, oh stag-boy come home!*

Tara Bergin

The Fox

Tree-silence, field-silence, snow-silence
welcome the fox to the edge of the plantation.
He is not surprised to see us
but nothing will break
that unblinking wariness. His narrow head
contains us, his eyes harbour the glint
of inhospitable winters. Nothing to be fearer or gained,

he takes himself off, loping close to the hedge,
his hollow stomach gathering a fringe of snow.
We plunge and scatter home to announce the fox.
Will he be back tonight in search of our kitchen waste?
Is he cunning enough to avoid the gamekeeper's traps?
We'll stay awake, listening for his bark.

Frank Ormsby

Swarm

Search for them in the canopy,
among meadow grasses,

you won't spot them;
the thousands of bees

that unzip the air,
follow the day's weft,

that rip the silence like cloth,
tug the tiny hairs on skin

with their ghost music –
bees long dead, bees soon to die,

as the ladder of evolution
reaches its vanishing point.

They hide here
among birdsfoot trefoil,

purple vetch, self-heal,
among hemlock and nightshade

and they wait,
these phantom bees,

between the dusty pines
with those who have

nothing to fear;
the numberless dead.

Jessica Traynor

Summer Yearn

It's almost dark in my bedroom,
outside the lake still glows.
If I could just slide from these covers
and lie in the tickling grass,
I'd eavesdrop on the crowd
readying for the night –
pulling on their fox trousers, badger coats,
heading for our neighbours' hills.
Hares on the beat, hedgehogs on the ball,
deer drinking long in the late night lake-bar.
Mink slink through brambles
as midnight's satin shifts from the east,
and a liquid dark slips over us all.

Eithne Hand

Hills and Mountains

The long and waving line of the blue hills
Makes rhythmical the twilight

from 'Peace', Eva Gore-Booth

Bilberry Blossom on Seefin

for J.

Halfway between mist and cloud,
we saw it by the barbed-wire fence –
pink-edged boxwood,
and the flowers, rosy cats' bells,
so round and waxy we took them for berries
but May is too early.
And after that there were low clumps everywhere,
the tiny bells secretive as nipples.
It bloomed through last year's heather
up near the summit,
where we unwrapped our sandwiches
as wind sheared through an empty tomb

and I imagine the bilberry-pickers
who used to climb the hills in August,
long-dead boys and girls –
cattle-herders, butter-makers,
singers, dancers – brash and shy
as any disco- or club-goer
and full of the tug of summer's long desire.

And on our way down, just across the path
from a storm-flayed swatch of pine
grew great clumps of the pink and green bushes.
And later still
as we drove down the mountain road
they grew tall along the verge,
so we pulled in and picked big bunches
to carry home
all the ringing promise
of that blossom and leaf
we had often seen before
but had never heard.

Moya Cannon

A Healing

That first day of springtime thaw when the ice
began to melt and pour down the mountains,
I walked to the top of the old mining road
to hear all the slow loosening and letting go;
the kick-back of copper and clay from my heels,
the steady blasts following like the sound
of another person's footfall on the shale,
spirited behind me; the stream that thundered
down to disappear again underground
so the whole place was all tremble and go,
lightening into a stiller and clearer air.
I loved the copper-lit, the downhill skid and slack,
the water roaring out of time, turning back
with so much sound and rush that it seemed
to be gathering strength from ore and dust and clay,
under the shade of that green and beaten ground.

Leanne O'Sullivan

Prelude

Still south I went and west and south again,
Through Wicklow from the morning till the night,
And far from cities, and the sites of men,
Lived with the sunshine and the moon's delight.

I knew the stars, the flowers, and the birds,
The grey and wintry sides of many glens,
And did but half remember human words,
In converse with the mountains, moors, and fens.

J.M. Synge

A Merlin in the Sheefrys

There is a feeling that is equal to the land,
a sense of self that is the journey's length.
It changes, bright to dark, and back again,
in moments such as when a hill decides
to vanish, prompting the sea to appear,
sun-thatched, sun-pregnant, sun-remonstrating,
before another bog-dividing mile
leads down to a stretch where abundant rock,
as if by words, or acts, elicits calm.
And then, in a mood of three mountains, you drive on,
the land's equal by free and strange degrees,
one for whom a merlin sighting proves a way
to push the day to absolute kinship.
The merlin declares: 'I have brought you here.'
To which madness the Sheeffry winds reply,
'Talk to the dead as you would to the living.
Address the living as if they were the dead.'

Martin Dyar

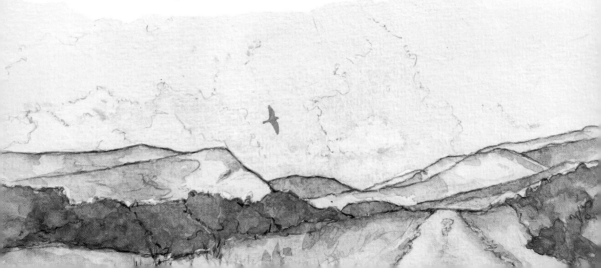

Border

At first I knew nothing of the border
or that I was being divided

from my own kind, women
who like me possess the earth

in their eyes,
the steep incline of mountains, valleys, wells.

Now, I trace the curves of shoulders,
in foundling photographs,

hems of hair that sweep towards the sun.
And I recall the plovers

on the heather-hill behind our house
each year, a cloak

of peat-gold wings flocking the sky
like mirrors.

Annemarie Ní Churreáin

The Land League

The Geological Survey in Ireland

Hard to keep one history from another,
but he kept his head low, used simple tools:
notebook and pencil and a good pair of boots,
and a lunch prepared in the boarding house
if the landlady was willing, which they
usually were, this being official scientific business.

Today, day three at the Gweebarra Fault.
Moorland; heather and moss; bold naked
granite bursting through. He takes the path
along the widening lake to Glenveagh,
learns from Mrs Adair about the last red
deer to leave Co. Donegal, not long back.

'Did you learn,' they'd ask him later in the pub,
'about Mr Adair, forcing out them families,
most now dead.' Hard to counter their talk
of agitation and freedom with limestone,
to explain how a glacier rolled down
this valley, flexured and folded the land.

Michael McKimm

Recipe for a Bog

Block the gullies and grips
    where the river rises,

slow the downhill flow
    of peat-filled streams.

Fell spruce and pine
    that thirst for moisture,

mulch parched earth
    with heather brash.

Graft sphagnum moss
    from healthy banks,

lay straw,
    feather-light on fragments.

Welcome rain,
    praise puddles

spreading into ponds.
    Count frogs.

Watch Emperor Moths
        in cotton grass,

a spider trapped
        on sundew tendrils,

dragonflies skittish
        from butterwort to asphodel
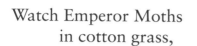

and a pair of low-flying merlin
        wingbeat, wingbeat, glide.

Jane Clarke

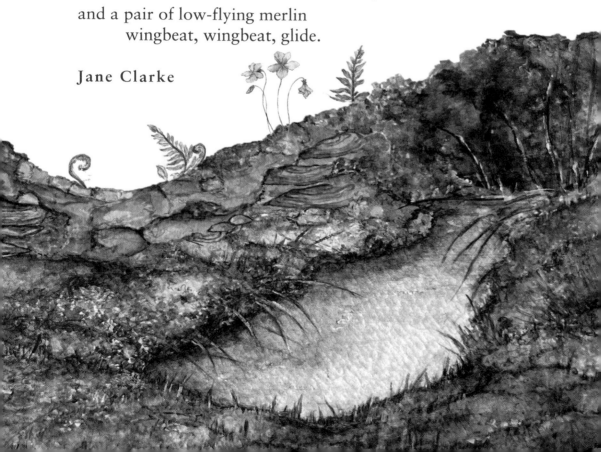

Black Mountain Viewed from English 6

Sometimes in the middle of a class we'll stop
and look out the window. It is the highest and
biggest in the school and framed by it is a sweep
of mountain that gives a sense of the west
of the city. The little streets become beautiful
geometry as the light catches identical parades
of chimneys grey below the mountain's green
and on the top a lazy orographic cloud
will lie along it in the morning until moved
or melted by the sun. And one day there's a fire
with the fireman up a ladder peeing his water
on a burning house and every so often a sun-burst
of white gulls will wheel upward lifting like a surprise
across the rooftops and the tall row of poplar trees
that bind the nuns' graveyard have been pollarded
stark against the winter sky and often weather
will roll in and down, rain bleaching all the colour
out to a grey blur, only for it to come back
in bright contrasts after the shower.

Maureen Boyle

Peace

The long and waving line of the blue hills
Makes rhythmical the twilight, no sharp peak
Pierces the kind air with a rough-hewn will
To storm the sky, no soaring mountains seek
To break the melody of the flowing line,
But the hills wander on in a long wave,
And all the while invisible stars shine
Over the sea and white cairn of Maeve.

Eva Gore-Booth

In the Garden

Stars rise.
Moths flutter.
Apples sweeten in the dark.

from 'This Moment', Eavan Boland

The Sunlight on the Garden

The sunlight on the garden
Hardens and grows cold,
We cannot cage the minute
Within its nets of gold,
When all is told
We cannot beg for pardon.

Our freedom as free lances
Advances towards its end;
The earth compels, upon it
Sonnets and birds descend;
And soon, my friend,
We shall have no time for dances.

The sky was good for flying
Defying the church bells
And every evil iron
Siren and what it tells:
The earth compels,
We are dying, Egypt, dying

And not expecting pardon,
Hardened in heart anew,
But glad to have sat under
Thunder and rain with you,
And grateful too
For sunlight on the garden.

Louis MacNeice

This Moment

A neighbourhood.
At dusk.

Things are getting ready
to happen
out of sight.

Stars and moths.
And rinds slanting around fruit.

But not yet.

One tree is black.
One window is yellow as butter.

A woman leans down to catch a child
who has run into her arms
this moment.

Stars rise.
Moths flutter.
Apples sweeten in the dark.

Eavan Boland

Seed

The first warm day of spring
and I step out into the garden from the gloom
of a house where hope had died
to tally the storm damage, to seek what may
have survived. And finding some forgotten
lupins I'd sown from seed last autumn
holding in their fingers a raindrop each
like a peace offering, or a promise,
I am suddenly grateful and would
offer a prayer if I believed in god.
But not believing, I bless the power of seed,
its casual, useful persistence,
and bless the power of sun,
its conspiracy with the underground,
and thank my stars the winter's ended.

Paula Meehan

Sea Garden

I'll go no further
than the low stone
wall, its rusted gate

leaning like a soldier
on a crutch. The wind
has dropped, sky's mouth

clapped shut, clothes
hang easy from the line.
This garden's space

enough to stage small
miracles: if I sit still
I'll see plants grow, hear

cells divide, stems
thicken and unfold
until earth's crust cracks,

leaves break through,
like seals' heads
surfacing to sun.

Geraldine Mitchell

Blackbird

for Ciarín, three months pregnant

The scissoring blades had come so close
That I almost sliced the nest and its three
Speckled blue eggs, suddenly and brutally
Exposed, balanced, on a few new shoots
Of the hedge I was cutting. And I thought
She would never return, that the nest
And eggs would shrivel away into a sad
Might have been. But less than an hour
Saw her brown tail again cocked over the nest,

Her yellow beak and accusing eye willing me
Not to betray her again, willing the wind
Not to capsize her world, willing the blades
To hold off awhile. And now a gale has come
And gone, and she is still sitting on the eggs,
And I am holding my breath day after day,
Willing her just a few more weeks of grace.

Paddy Bushe

Worm

Burrowing in your allotted patch you
move through the dark, muscles contracting one by one

in every part, lengthening and shortening
the slick segmented tube of you, furrows in your wake.

Devising passages for water, air,
you plot the gaps that keep the structure from collapse.

Dead things you know. Plants and creatures both.
Your grooves shift matter, sifting as you go.

Eyeless, your appetite aerates.
Eating the world, you open it.

You ingest to differentiate.
Under the foot-stamped earth, you eat into a clot

of leaf mould, clay and mildew, and express what you can
part with, as self-possessed as when you started.

Your secretions bind the soil,
your shit enriches it. How things lie

now will be undone, will reoccur. You, a surface-level archivist
sensing all there is

can be gone through. The body borne
within its plot.

Gail McConnell

Polygonum Baldschuanicum

(Colloquial names: 'Russian Vine' or 'Mile-a-Minute')

One day it shall be you who will inherit
     Every house and shed and each crevice
Leading to every penthouse, lift-shaft or billet.

Rooftops of tangled blossoms entwining,
     Tendrils glistening in rooms
That light and voices have long forsaken.

No place will have escaped your noose
     Of leaves and shoots; a green python
Choking our civilization: this dozing goose,
     Who forgot to sleep with one eye open.

Dermot Bolger

The Red Gate

Mornings, when you swing open the red gate –
admitting the world again with its creeds and wars –
the hinges sing their three sharp notes of protest;
you hear the poplars in their murmurings and sifflings
while the labouring high caravans of the rain
pass slowly by; it will seem as if the old
certainties of the moon and stars, mingled
with the turnings and returnings of your dreams, mist
to unreality, although there rise about you
matins and lauds of the meadowsweet and rowan; the first
truck goes ruttling down the wet road and the raw
arguments, the self-betrayed economies of governments
assault you so you may miss the clear-souled drops
on the topmost bar that would whisper you peace.

John F. Deane

The Land

It was about the little fields
That call across the world to me.

from 'Home', Francis Ledwidge

Woman Shoeing a Horse

This is the path to the stile
and this is where I would stand –
the place is all thick with weeds.

I could see the line of her back and the flash of her hair
as she came from the fields at a call,
and then ten minutes wasted, all quiet

but the horse in the open air clanking his feet
until the fire was roaring and the work began,
and the clattering and dancing.

I could see by her shoulders how her breath shifted
in the burst of the heat, and the wide gesture of her free arm
as she lifted the weight and clung

around the hoof. The hammer notes were flying
all urgent with fire and speed, and precise
with a finicky catch at the end –

but the noise I could not hear was the shock of air
crashing into her lungs, the depth
of the gasp as she turned with a ready hand

as the heat from the fire drew up the chimney,
the flame pressing, brushing out the last thread,
constantly revising itself upwards to a pure line.

I close my eyes, not to see the rider as he left.
When I opened them again the sheep were
    inching forward,
a flock of starlings had darkened the sky.

Eiléan Ní Chuilleanáin

To the Man After the Harrow

Now leave the check-reins slack,
The seed is flying far today –
The seed like stars against the black
Eternity of April clay.

This seed is potent as the seed
Of knowledge in the Hebrew Book,
So drive your horses in the creed
Of God the Father as a stook.

Forget the men on Brady's Hill.
Forget what Brady's boy may say.
For destiny will not fulfil
Unless you let the harrow play.

Forget the worm's opinion too
Of hooves and pointed harrow-pins,
For you are driving your horses through
The mist where Genesis begins.

Patrick Kavanagh

The Lost Heifer

When the black herds of the rain were grazing,
In the gap of the pure cold wind
And the watery hazes of the hazel
Brought her into my mind,
I thought of the last honey by the water
That no hive can find.

Brightness was drenching through the branches
When she wandered again,
Turning the silver out of dark grasses
Where the skylark had lain,
And her voice coming softly over the meadow
Was the mist becoming rain.

Austin Clarke

For My Grandmother, Bridget Halpin

Maybe morning lightens over
the coldest time in all the day,
but not for you. A bird's hover,
seabird, blackbird, or bird of prey,
was rain, or death, or lost cattle.
The day's warning, like red plovers so
etched and small the clouded sky, was
book to you, and true bible. You died
in utter loneliness,
your acres left to the childless.
You never saw the animals
of God, and the flower under
your feet; and the trees change a leaf;
and the red fur of a fox on
a quiet evening; and the long
birches falling down the hillside.

Michael Hartnett

Bolus Head Sonata

Unlikely looking gift, this five-barred,
metal gate, rusting, crossed,
tethered in its lock by blue nylon strings.
The signs unwelcoming: dogs beware,
walkers climb at their peril
in this kingdom of scrub and rock.

But if you hold your ground,
if the wind is in the right direction,
the gate will sing to you,
notes seemingly haphazard
unless you wait for a pattern.

doh soh fah doh
lah soh fah doh

Contrapuntal recitative, hollow,
a blast of close encounters,
than a lull so long
you think you have imagined it
until it begins again, the same lilt,
the same scaling heights,
a luthier's delight.

A chough breaks in,
his bass notes have no role
in this tubular belling
as it funnels wind,
revolves it into tune again

and again

and again.

Nessa O'Mahony

Up the Border

If they come asking , tell them I've gone to walk the border,
where eight-year-olds used to know how to smuggle diesel
past the dragon's teeth, where one field opens onto another,

and a fly-tipped fridge might bristle a ribcage of bluebells,
and you're as like to find schoolkids taking a feed of cider
as a hush of forty-year-olds urging bloodlust from pitbulls,

where hedges hide porn and barbed wire dangles knickers,
and Nelis swears he once got a girl fresh out of Marseilles
to stretch bareback on the tarmac in the middle of summer,

and the winter the Foyle froze over, submerged to its middle,
he found a fox in the shuck, its entrails and spine uncovered
by jackdaws, ear-tufts and tail-tip blooming out of a puddle

and even though its small face was frozen intact underwater,
he got the sense that if he hacked out and thawed its pupils,
they'd be sharp as lasers with the focus of crossing over.

Eoghan Walls

Deep Ulster

It was there, the elemental centre,
All the time. Eternally present, repeating itself
Like seasons, where the times and dates
For swallows and household fires are written down,

The grouse are counted, the quotas of stocked rainbows.
All that love of order, for its own sake.
Only the hill-farms, and the high sheep country
Above politics–the enormous relief

Up there, as the dialect names of skies
Return, along with their clouds, and the old knowledge
Opens the mind again. To dream, to just potter
In the yard, to fiddle with local stations

In the kitchen, where news that is no news
Finally, at last, fills up the years
With pure existence. Lit from beneath
The fields are evenings long, the tree by the house

Where Vladimir and Estragon kept vigil
With the stillness of commando and insurgent
Frightens no one. Slow through the air
A heron, shouldering aside the weight of the world,

Is making for its colonies, coevals
In a state plantation . . .
                              Nowhere but here
In the high right hand of Ireland, do the weather-fronts
Give way so slowly, to such ambivalent light.

Harry Clifton

Grass

Grass, I've been watching you,
so slow to turn from winter to spring,

then growth green and low,
pushing up your language
of spikelet and seed-head,

soft, blowsy, tufted,
florets and anthers and awns.

A plenitude. A beatitude.
Some old religious word
for abundance and beauty combined,

but nothing lofty,
just grass,

fescue, scutch, timothy,
dog's tail, fox tail,
hard-grass, hair-grass, heath.

Where grain begins.
Where it all begins,

down in the grass.

Grace Wells

Why Brownlee Left

Why Brownlee left, and where he went,
Is a mystery even now.
For if a man should have been content
It was him; two acres of barley,
One of potatoes, four bullocks,
A milker, a slated farmhouse.
He was last seen going out to plough
On a March morning, bright and early.

By noon Brownlee was famous;
They had found all abandoned, with
The last rig unbroken, his pair of black
Horses, like man and wife,
Shifting their weight from foot to
Foot, and gazing into the future.

Paul Muldoon

Reaper-and-Binder

Voices were lost as the reaper-and-binder
Went clacketing past, spitting out at you showers
Of gold you embraced with your arms overfull,
So the sheaves slithered down from the grip of their
    bindings
As children, incompetent, slide out of jumpers.

At night on your pillow your ears went on singing
In time to its music by echo and echo
While your awn-scalded forearms still throbbed from
    its fallout.

Bernard O'Donoghue

Roscommon Rain

When the rain stopped the rain began
And clattered beads of runny light against the panes
Decreased and crept inside the ghosts of sheep
And seeped inside the warmth of prostrate cows.
Then pelted bogs to syrupy peat
Made gravelly lanes glitter again
Beneath the melting greys of cloud and cloud
Pierced the puddles with a thousand stings
Tumbled silver through the hedges
And off the skinned shin-bones of trees;
Swept, soft again, like a haze of locusts
Across the ridge, then shifted shape in sudden wind
Drifting, finer than chimney smoke,
Like a passing pang of some great loss
Away from where more rain was coming in
From somewhere else beyond the world's rim
Erasing gradually the misconception
That the world had ever not been rain
And rain would cease before the end of time.

James Harpur

Home

A burst of sudden wings at dawn,
Faint voices in a dreamy noon,
Evenings of mist and murmurings,
And nights with rainbows of the moon.

And through these things a wood-way dim,
And waters dim, and slow sheep seen
On uphill paths that wind away
Through summer sounds and harvest green.

This is a song a robin sang
This morning on a broken tree,
It was about the little fields
That call across the world to me.

Belgium,
July, 1917.

Francis Ledwidge

Acknowledgements

My gratitude to the poets for their enthusiasm and generosity about the inclusion of their work in this anthology.

Heartfelt thanks to Ciara Considine in Hachette Books Ireland who approached us with the idea for this anthology and shepherded it into being with vision, dedication and care.

Particular thanks to the superbly talented Jane Carkill with whom it was a pleasure to collaborate, and to Olivia O'Leary for generously providing the foreword to the book.

Many thanks to Neil Hegarty, Kerrie O'Brien, Dave O'Grady, Geraldine Mitchell, Katie Donovan, Nessa O'Mahony, Andrew Clarke and Isobel O'Duffy whose advice along the way made all the difference.

– Jane Clarke

Thanks to friends and family, for their unwavering encouragement and support for all that I create.

The team at Hachette publishing, especially publisher and editor Ciara Considine, for her gentle guidance and care that has helped Jane Clarke and I bring our vision to life.

To Jane Clarke, for your brilliant curation and counselling me along the journey through interpretation and giving these chosen words a deserving representation.

For Marian O'Callaghan, who many years ago ignited within me a love and appreciation for poetry that is still ever present to this day.

– Jane Carkill

Poem Acknowledgements

Amanda Bell's 'Riptide' is reprinted from *Riptide* by Amanda Bell (Doire Press, 2021), by kind permission of Doire Press.

Tara Bergin's 'Stag-Boy' is reprinted from *This is Yarrow* by Tara Bergin (Carcanet Press, 2013), by kind permission of Carcanet Press.

Eavan Boland's 'This Moment' is reprinted from *New Collected Poems* by Eavan Boland (Carcanet Press/W. W. Norton, 2012), by kind permission of Carcanet Press in the UK and W. W. Norton in the US.

Dermot Bolger's 'Polygonum Baldschuanicum' is reprinted from *That Which is Suddenly Precious: New & Selected Poems* by Dermot Bolger (New Island Books, 2015), by kind permission of the author.

Maureen Boyle's 'Black Mountain Viewed from English 6' is reprinted from *The Work of a Winter* by Maureen Boyle (Arlen House, 2018), by kind permission of Arlen House.

Paddy Bushe's 'Blackbird' is reprinted from *The Word Ark: A Pocket Book of Animal Poems*, edited by Pat Boran (Dedalus Press, 2020), by kind permission of Dedalus Press.

Siobhán Campbell's 'Longboat at Portaferry' was first published in New Hibernia Review and is reprinted by kind permission of the author.

Moya Cannon's 'Bilberry Blossom on Seefin' is reprinted from *Keats Lives* by Moya Cannon (Carcanet Press 2015), by kind permission of Carcanet Press.

Austin Clarke's 'The Lost Heifer' is reprinted from *Collected Poems*, edited by R. Dardis Clarke (Carcanet Press, 2008), by kind permission of Carcanet Press.

Jane Clarke's 'Recipe for a Bog' is reprinted from *A Change in the Air* by Jane Clarke (Bloodaxe Books, 2023), by kind permission of Bloodaxe Books.

Harry Clifton's 'Deep Ulster' is reprinted from *The Winter Sleep of Captain Lemass* by Harry Clifton (Bloodaxe Books, 2012), by kind permission of Bloodaxe Books.

John F. Deane's 'The Red Gate' is reprinted from *Snow Falling on Chestnut Hill: New and Selected Poems* by John F. Deane (Carcanet Press, 2012), by kind permission of Carcanet Press.

Katie Donovan's 'Cows' is reprinted from *Rootling: New & Selected* by Katie Donovan (Bloodaxe Books, 2010), by kind permission of Bloodaxe Books.

Paul Durcan's 'Staring Out the Window Three Weeks After His Death' is reprinted from *Praise in Which I Live and Move and Have my Being* by Paul Durcan (Harvill Secker, 2012), by kind permission of RCW Literary Agency.

Martin Dyar's 'A Merlin in the Sheefrys' is reprinted from *The Meek* by Martin Dyar (Wake Forest University Press, 2023), by kind permission of Wake Forest University Press.

Nidhi Zak/Aria Eipe's 'wandersong' is reprinted by kind permission of the author.

Tom French's 'A Plum Tree' is reprinted from *Midnightstown* by Tom French (Gallery Press, 2014), by kind permission of Gallery Press.

Miriam Gamble's 'Mare at Large' is reprinted from *What Planet* by Miriam Gamble (Bloodaxe Books, 2019), by kind permission of Bloodaxe Books.

Eva Gore-Booth's 'Peace' is reprinted from *The One and the Many* by Eva Gore-Booth (Longmans, Green, and Co., 1904).

Kevin Graham's 'The Lesson' is reprinted from *The Lookout Post* by Kevin Graham (Gallery Press, 2023), by kind permission of Gallery Press.

Eamon Grennan's 'Trees Abiding' is reprinted from *There Now* by Eamon Grennan (Gallery Press, 2015), by kind permission of Gallery Press.

Vona Groarke's 'Pier' is reprinted from *Spindrift* by Vona Groarke (Gallery Press, 2009), by kind permission of Gallery Press.

Eithne Hand's 'Summer Yearn' is reprinted from *Fox Trousers* by Eithne Hand (Salmon Poetry, 2020), by kind permission of Salmon Poetry.

James Harpur's 'Roscommon Rain' is reprinted from *The Dark Age* by James Harpur (Anvil Press, 2007) by kind permission of the author.

Michael Hartnett's 'For My Grandmother, Bridget Halpin' is reprinted from *Collected Poems* by Michael Hartnett (Gallery Press, 2001), by kind permission of Gallery Press.

Francis Harvey's 'Heron' is reprinted from *Collected Poems* by Francis Harvey (Dedalus Press, 2007), by kind permission of Dedalus Press.

Dermot Healy's 'The Five Senses' is reprinted from *Collected Poems* by Dermot Healey (Gallery Press, 2018), by kind permission of Gallery Press.

Seamus Heaney's 'Planting the Alder' is reprinted from *District and Circle* by Seamus Heaney (Faber & Faber, 2006), by kind permission of Faber and Faber Ltd in the UK. For US rights: 'Planting the Alder' from *District and Circle* by Seamus Heaney. Copyright © 2006 by Seamus Heaney. Reprinted by permission of Farrar, Straus and Giroux. All Rights Reserved.

John Hewitt's 'The Watchers' is reprinted from *The Selected Poems of John Hewitt*, edited by Michael Longley and Frank Ormsby (Blackstaff Press, 2007), by kind permission of Blackstaff Press.

Seán Hewitt's 'Wild Garlic' is reprinted From *Tongues of Fire* by Seán Hewitt published by Vintage Digital. Copyright © Seán Hewitt, 2020. Reprinted by permission of Penguin Books Limited.

Eleanor Hooker's 'The Quicken Tree' is reprinted from *Of Ochre and Ash* by Eleanor Hooker (Dedalus Press, 2021), by kind permission of Dedalus Press.

Patrick Kavanagh's 'To the Man After the Harrow' is reprinted from *Collected Poems*, edited by Antoinette Quinn (Allen Lane, 2004), by kind permission of the Trustees of the Estate of the late Katherine B. Kavanagh, through the Jonathan Williams Literary Agency.

Nick Laird's 'Night Sky in Tyrone' is reprinted from *Up Late* by Nick Laird (Faber & Faber/W. W. Norton, 2023), by kind permission of Faber and Faber Ltd in the UK and W. W. Norton in the US.

Freda Laughton's 'Now Linnet' is reprinted from *Transitory House* by Freda Laughton published by Jonathan Cape. Copyright © Freda Laughton, 1945. Reprinted by permission of Penguin Books Limited.

Francis Ledwidge's 'Home' is reprinted from *Selected Poems*, edited by Dermot Bolger (New Island, 2001).

Winifred M. Letts's 'Dead' is reprinted from *Hallow-e'en and Poems of the War* by Winifred M. Letts (John Murray, 1916), by kind permission of Oriana Conner.

Michael Longley's 'The Leveret' is reprinted from *A Hundred Doors* by Michael Longley published by Jonathan Cape. Copyright © Michael Longley, 2011. Reprinted by permission of Penguin Books Limited.

Aoife Lyall's 'Month's Mind' is reprinted from *Mother Nature* by Aoife Lyall (Bloodaxe Books, 2021), by kind permission of Bloodaxe Books.

Richard Murphy's 'Seals at High Island' is reprinted from *Collected Poems 1952–2000* by Richard Murphy (Wake Forest University Press/Bloodaxe Books/Lilliput Press, 2001/2013), by kind permission of Wake Forest University Press in the US, Bloodaxe Books in the UK, and Lilliput Press in Ireland.

Eiléan Ní Chuilleanáin's 'Woman Shoeing a Horse' is reprinted from *The Brazen Serpent* by Eiléan Ní Chuilleanáin (Gallery Press, 1994), by kind permission of Gallery Press.

Annemarie Ní Churreáin's 'Border' is reprinted from *Bloodroot* by Annemarie Ní Churreáin (Doire Press, 2017), by kind permission of Doire Press.

Nuala Ní Dhomhnaill's 'Leaba Shíoda' and 'Labbysheedy' are reprinted from *Selected Poems: Rogha Dánta* by Nuala Ní Dhomhnaill (New Island Books, 2004), by kind permission of the author.

Doireann Ní Ghríofa's 'Fáinleoga & Swallows' is reprinted from *Lies* by Doireann Ní Ghríofa (Dedalus Press, 2018), by kind permission of Dedalus Press.

Joseph O'Connor's 'Blackbird in Dun Laoghaire' is reprinted by kind permission of the author.

Bernard O'Donoghue's 'Reaper-and-Binder' is reprinted from *Selected Poems* by Bernard O'Donoghue (Faber & Faber, 2008), by kind permission of the author.

Nessa O'Mahony's 'Bolus Head Sonata' is reprinted from *The Hollow Woman on the Island* by Nessa O'Mahony (Salmon Poetry, 2019), by kind permission of Salmon Poetry.

Mary O'Malley's 'Tree III' is reprinted from *Playing the Octopus* by Mary O'Malley (Carcanet Press, 2016), by kind permission of Carcanet Press.

Caitríona O'Reilly's 'Octopus' is reprinted from *The Nowhere Birds* by Caitríona O'Reilly (Bloodaxe Books, 2001), by kind permission of Bloodaxe Books.

Frank Ormsby's 'The Fox' is reprinted from *The Darkness of Snow* by Frank Ormsby (Bloodaxe Books, 2017), by kind permission of Bloodaxe Books.

Leanne O'Sullivan's 'A Healing' is reprinted from *The Mining Road* by Leanne O'Sullivan (Bloodaxe Books, 2013), by kind permission of Bloodaxe Books.

Jane Robinson's 'The Waste Land Recovers' is reprinted from *Island and Atoll* by Jane Robinson (Salmon Poetry, 2023), by kind permission of Salmon Poetry.

Mark Roper's 'Owl' is reprinted from *Beyond Stillness* by Mark Roper (Dedalus Press, 2022), by kind permission of Dedalus Press.

John M. Synge's 'Prelude' is reprinted from *Poems and Translations* by John Millington Synge (Cuala Press, 1909).

Rosamund Taylor's 'The Drey' is reprinted from *In Her Jaws* by Rosamund Taylor (Banshee Press, 2022), by kind permission of Banshee Press.

Jessica Traynor's 'Swarm' is reprinted from *The Quick* by Jessica Traynor (Dedalus Press, 2018), by kind permission of Dedalus Press.

Eoghan Walls's 'Up the Border' is reprinted from *Pigeon Songs* (Seren Books, 2019), by kind permission of Seren Books.

Grace Wells's 'Grass' is reprinted from *The Church of the Love of the World* by Grace Wells (Dedalus Press, 2022), by kind permission of Dedalus Press.

W. B. Yeats's 'The Song of Wandering Aengus' is reprinted from *The Wind Among the Reeds* by W. B. Yeats (Elkin Mathews, 1899).